W9-CGR-264

Animals in Their Habitats

Rain Forest Animals

Francine Galko

Heinemann Library
Chicago, Illinois

© 2003 Reed Educational & Professional Publishing
Published by Heinemann Library,
an imprint of Capstone Global Library, LLC
Chicago, Illinois
Customer Service 888-454-2279
Visit our website at www.heinemannlibrary.com

All rights reserved. No part of this publication may be reproduced or transmitted in any form or by any means, electronic or mechanical, including photocopying, recording, taping, or any information storage and retrieval system, without permission in writing from the publisher.

Designed by Ginkgo Creative
Printed in the United States of America in Stevens Point, Wisconsin.   062013   007564R

Library of Congress Cataloging-in-Publication Data

Galko, Francine.
   Rainforest animals / Francine Galko.
      p. cm. — (Animals and their habitats)
Summary: Explores the animals that make their habitat in the rainforest.
Includes bibliographical references (p.   ).
   ISBN 10: 1-4034-0182-9 (HB), 1-4034-0439-9 (Pbk)
   ISBN 13: 978-1-4034-1082-3 (HB), 978-1-4034-0439-8 (Pbk)
   1. Rain forest animals—Juvenile literature. 2. Rain forests—Juvenile literature. [1. Rain forest animals.] I. Title.
   QL112 .G25 2002
   591.734—dc21
                           2001007658

Acknowledgments
The author and publishers are grateful to the following for permission to reproduce copyright material:
Cover photograph by Kevin Schafer
p. 4 Janis Burger/Bruce Coleman Inc.; pp. 5, 10 Michael Fogden/Bruce Coleman Inc.; pp. 6, 7, 9, 11, 14 Kevin Schafer; p. 8 Dani/Jeske/Animals Animals; p. 12 Tom Brakefield/Bruce Coleman Inc.; p. 13 David Dennis/Animals Animals; p. 15 John Pontier/Animals Animals; p. 16 Tui de Roy/Minden Pictures; p. 17 Doug Wechsler/Animals Animals; p. 18 Norman Owen Tomalin/Bruce Coleman Inc.; p. 19 Erwin and Peggy Bauer; p. 20 H.L. Fox OSF/Animals Animals; p. 21 Candice Bayer/Bruce Coleman Inc.; p. 22 Frans Lanting/Minden Pictures; p. 23 Gerard Lacz/Animals Animals; p. 24 Michael Fogden/Animals Animals; p. 25 M. Fogden/OSF/Animals Animals; p. 26 Oxford Scientific Films; p. 27 A. Root/OSF/Animals Animals; p. 28 Juan Manuel Renjifo/Animals Animals; p. 29 Michael Dick/Animals Animals
Every effort has been made to contact copyright holders of any material reproduced in this book. Any omissions will be rectified in subsequent printings if notice is given to the publisher.

Some words are shown in bold, **like this.** You can find out what they mean by looking in the glossary.

To learn more about the arrow-poison frog on the cover, turn to page 9.

Contents

What is a Rain Forest?

A rain forest is a kind of **habitat.** It is a place with many tall trees. Rain forests are wet and warm most of the time. Rain falls often in some rain forests.

In **lowland rain forests,** a nearby river sometimes **floods** the land with water. In the mountains, clouds touch the tops of the trees. Instead of rain, the clouds make **mist.**

Where are Rain Forests?

Rain forests cover a small part of Earth. They are not found everywhere. They usually grow on or near the **equator**. That is one reason they are so special.

Plants and animals grow well in the summerlike weather near the equator. Rain forests have more plants and animals than most other places do.

Rain Forest Homes

Rain forests have many places for animals to live. Sloths spend most of their time hanging upside down high up in the trees. They use their claws to hang on to branches and they eat leaves.

This arrow-poison frog lives on the rain forest floor. Its bright color tells other animals that it is a **poisonous** frog.

Living on the Rain Forest Floor

It's dark on the rain forest floor. The tall trees keep the sun out. Down here, tapirs eat different kinds of plants. They usually live near a river in the rain forest.

Leaf-cutter ants also live on the rain forest floor. These ants cut plant leaves with their sharp jaws. Then they carry the leaves back to their underground **nests.**

Living in the Understory

Young trees and the trunks of very tall trees make up the **understory**. This is the middle layer of the rain forest. Here, jaguars climb trees and watch for **prey** on the ground.

Giant cockroaches live in the trees and leaves of the rain forest understory. A full-grown giant cockroach is bigger than your hand.

Living in the Canopy

The **canopy** is the top of the rain forest. Here, the tops of very tall trees grow close together. Toucans make their homes in the rain forest canopy.

Spider monkeys also live in the canopy. These monkeys use their hands to swing through the trees. They can also hang upside down by their tail.

Living on Top of the Trees

The harpy eagle lives at the top of the tallest trees. It catches monkeys and other tree animals for food.

Cacique (ka•seek) birds hang their nests from tree branches. These birds eat fruit and insects from the trees. They can also catch flying termites.

Finding Food in a Rain Forest

Rain forests have many plants and small animals to eat. Shiny, blue morpho butterflies drink **nectar** from rain forest flowers.

Green iguanas are lizards. They live in rain forest trees and eat lots of plants. Sometimes they wait in the tree branches until insects come along. Then they eat the insects.

Rain Forest Predators

Many rain forest animals are **predators.**
Trap-door spiders wait in their underground
holes for **prey** to walk by. Then they quickly
open their trap door, catch the prey, and
take it into their hole.

Anaconda snakes live in rain forest rivers and swamps. They wait in the water for prey. Then they wrap themselves around the animal and squeeze tight.

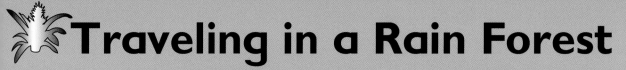

Parrots, like this macaw, have strong wings to fly fast through the forest. They use their strong nails to hold on to the tree branches.

Woolly monkeys move through the rain forest using their hands, feet, and tail. Their toes and thumbs help them hold on to tree branches.

Hiding in a Rain Forest

Camouflage is one way to hide from predators. Can you find the green praying mantis? It looks just like a leaf.

The long, thin vine snake looks like a **vine**. It lives in the branches of rain forest trees where it can hide from other animals.

Rain Forest Babies

Many baby animals live in the rain forest. Mother hummingbirds lay eggs in a tiny nest. When the eggs hatch, the baby birds will stay in the same rain forest.

A mother anteater will often carry her baby on her back. Sometimes she will put the baby on a tree branch while she gets food.

Protecting Rain Forest Animals

Sometimes people cut down all the trees in rain forests to make farms. But the land gets dry, and the rain washes away the dirt. Nothing can grow there anymore.

Rain forest animals like this tarsier (tar•see•er) need trees and water. Today, people know that only rain forest plants grow in rain forest dirt. Taking care of rain forests **protects** the animals that live there.

# Glossary

camouflage way an animal hides itself

canopy branches of trees at the top of a rain forest

equator imaginary line that divides the Earth in half

flood cover the land with water

habitat place where an animal lives

insect small animal with six legs

lowland rain forest rain forest that is sometimes covered with water from a nearby river

mist wet air

nectar sweet liquid found in some kinds of flowers

nest kind of animal home

poisonous harmful

predator animal that hunts and eats other animals

prey animal that is hunted and eaten by another animal

understory middle layer of a rain forest. The understory is made up of young trees and the trunks of very tall trees

vine thin plant stems that hang on other plants

More Books to Read

Arnosky, Jim. *Crinkleroot's Guide to Knowing Animal Habitats.* New York: Aladdin Picture Books, 1998.

Eugene, Tony. *Hide and Seek.* Washington, D.C.: National Geographic Society, 1999.

Fowler, Allan. *Save the Rain forests.* Danbury Conn.: Children's Press, 1996.

Gibbons, Gail. *Nature's Green Umbrella: Tropical Rain Forests.* Mulberry Books, 1997.

Silver, Donald M. and Patricia J. Wynne. *Tropical Rain Forest (One Small Square).* Columbus, Ohio: McGraw-Hill, 1998.

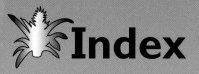# Index